IN MY BLOOD

FEATURED IN THE NETFLIX SERIES
BRIDGERTON

ORIGINALLY RECORDED BY
SHAWN MENDES

WORDS AND MUSIC BY
SHAWN MENDES, GEOFF WARBURTON, TEDDY GEIGER AND SCOTT HARRIS

AS ARRANGED BY KATHY McMILLEN FOR
VITAMIN STRING QUARTET

ISBN 978-1-7051-3465-8

Vitamin String Quartet

DISTRIBUTED BY

Visit Hal Leonard Online at
www.halleonard.com

Contact us:
Hal Leonard
7777 West Bluemound Road
Milwaukee, WI 53213
Email: info@halleonard.com

In Europe, contact:
Hal Leonard Europe Limited
42 Wigmore Street
Marylebone, London, W1U 2RN
Email: info@halleonardeurope.com

In Australia, contact:
Hal Leonard Australia Pty. Ltd.
4 Lentara Court
Cheltenham, Victoria, 3192 Australia
Email: info@halleonard.com.au

IN MY BLOOD

Words and Music by
Shawn Mendes, Geoff Warburton,
Teddy Geiger and Scott Harris
As arranged by Kathy McMillen
for Vitamin String Quartet

IN MY BLOOD

FEATURED IN THE NETFLIX SERIES
BRIDGERTON

ORIGINALLY RECORDED BY
SHAWN MENDES

WORDS AND MUSIC BY
SHAWN MENDES, GEOFF WARBURTON, TEDDY GEIGER AND SCOTT HARRIS

AS ARRANGED BY KATHY MCMILLEN FOR
VITAMIN STRING QUARTET

ISBN 978-1-7051-3465-8

Visit Hal Leonard Online at
www.halleonard.com

Contact us:
Hal Leonard
7777 West Bluemound Road
Milwaukee, WI 53213
Email: info@halleonard.com

In Europe, contact:
Hal Leonard Europe Limited
42 Wigmore Street
Marylebone, London, W1U 2RN
Email: info@halleonardeurope.com

In Australia, contact:
Hal Leonard Australia Pty. Ltd.
4 Lentara Court
Cheltenham, Victoria, 3192 Australia
Email: info@halleonard.com.au

IN MY BLOOD

Words and Music by
Shawn Mendes, Geoff Warburton,
Teddy Geiger and Scott Harris
As arranged by Kathy McMillen
for Vitamin String Quartet

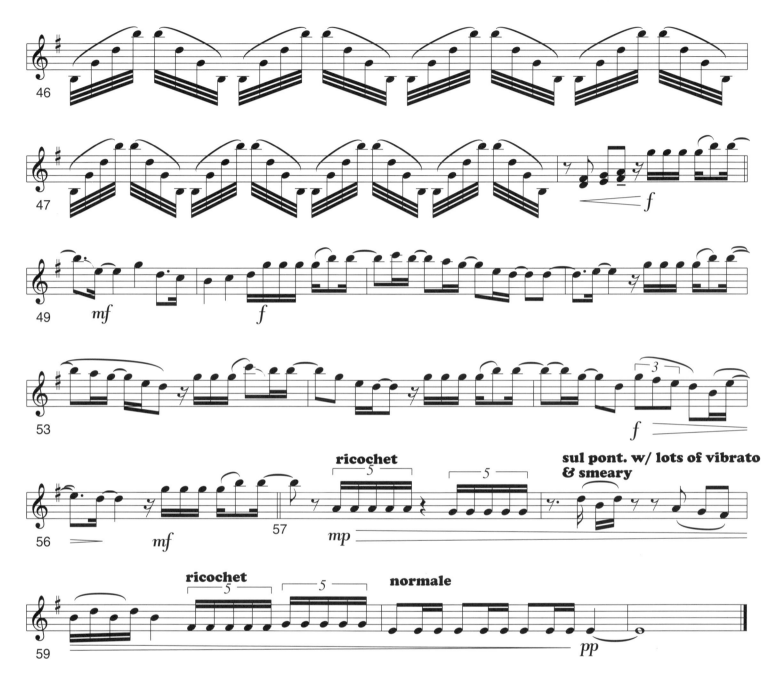

IN MY BLOOD

FEATURED IN THE NETFLIX SERIES
BRIDGERTON

ORIGINALLY RECORDED BY
SHAWN MENDES

WORDS AND MUSIC BY
SHAWN MENDES, GEOFF WARBURTON, TEDDY GEIGER AND SCOTT HARRIS

AS ARRANGED BY KATHY McMILLEN FOR
VITAMIN STRING QUARTET

ISBN 978-1-7051-3465-8

VSQ
Vitamin String Quartet

DISTRIBUTED BY

Hal•Leonard®

Visit Hal Leonard Online at
www.halleonard.com

Contact us:
Hal Leonard
7777 West Bluemound Road
Milwaukee, WI 53213
Email: info@halleonard.com

In Europe, contact:
Hal Leonard Europe Limited
42 Wigmore Street
Marylebone, London, W1U 2RN
Email: info@halleonardeurope.com

In Australia, contact:
Hal Leonard Australia Pty. Ltd.
4 Lentara Court
Cheltenham, Victoria, 3192 Australia
Email: info@halleonard.com.au

IN MY BLOOD

**Words and Music by
Shawn Mendes, Geoff Warburton,
Teddy Geiger and Scott Harris
As arranged by Kathy McMillen
for Vitamin String Quartet**

3

IN MY BLOOD

FEATURED IN THE NETFLIX SERIES
BRIDGERTON

ORIGINALLY RECORDED BY
SHAWN MENDES

WORDS AND MUSIC BY
SHAWN MENDES, GEOFF WARBURTON, TEDDY GEIGER AND SCOTT HARRIS

AS ARRANGED BY KATHY MCMILLEN FOR
VITAMIN STRING QUARTET

ISBN 978-1-7051-3465-8

Vitamin String Quartet

DISTRIBUTED BY

Visit Hal Leonard Online at
www.halleonard.com

Contact us:
Hal Leonard
7777 West Bluemound Road
Milwaukee, WI 53213
Email: info@halleonard.com

In Europe, contact:
Hal Leonard Europe Limited
42 Wigmore Street
Marylebone, London, W1U 2RN
Email: info@halleonardeurope.com

In Australia, contact:
Hal Leonard Australia Pty. Ltd.
4 Lentara Court
Cheltenham, Victoria, 3192 Australia
Email: info@halleonard.com.au

VIOLA

IN MY BLOOD

Words and Music by
Shawn Mendes, Geoff Warburton,
Teddy Geiger and Scott Harris
As arranged by Kathy McMillen
for Vitamin String Quartet

IN MY BLOOD

FEATURED IN THE NETFLIX SERIES
BRIDGERTON

ORIGINALLY RECORDED BY
SHAWN MENDES

WORDS AND MUSIC BY
SHAWN MENDES, GEOFF WARBURTON, TEDDY GEIGER AND SCOTT HARRIS

AS ARRANGED BY KATHY MCMILLEN FOR
VITAMIN STRING QUARTET

ISBN 978-1-7051-3465-8

DISTRIBUTED BY
HAL•LEONARD®

Visit Hal Leonard Online at
www.halleonard.com

Contact us:
Hal Leonard
7777 West Bluemound Road
Milwaukee, WI 53213
Email: info@halleonard.com

In Europe, contact:
Hal Leonard Europe Limited
42 Wigmore Street
Marylebone, London, W1U 2RN
Email: info@halleonardeurope.com

In Australia, contact:
Hal Leonard Australia Pty. Ltd.
4 Lentara Court
Cheltenham, Victoria, 3192 Australia
Email: info@halleonard.com.au

CELLO

IN MY BLOOD

Words and Music by
Shawn Mendes, Geoff Warburton,
Teddy Geiger and Scott Harris
As arranged by Kathy McMillen
for Vitamin String Quartet

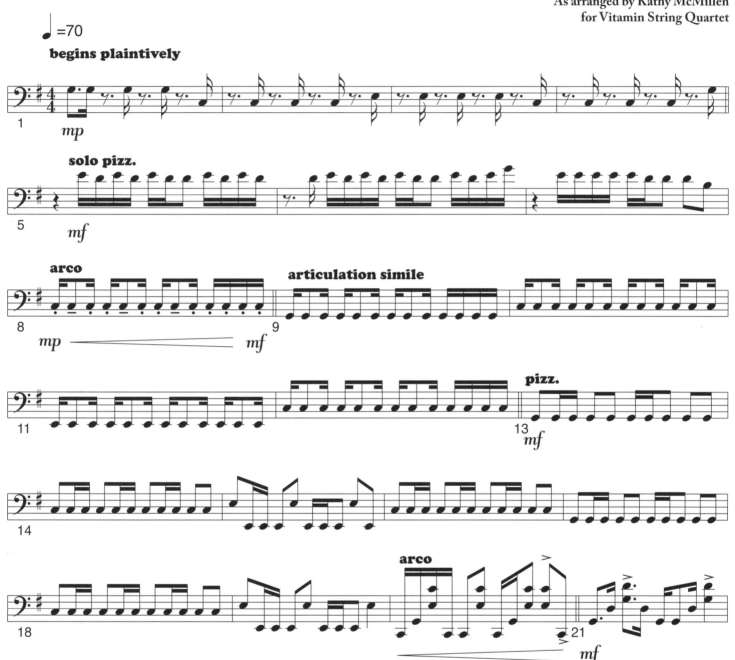

5